DO YOU REALLY WANT TO MEET A TIGER?

WRITTEN BY CARI MEISTER   ILLUSTRATED BY DANIELE FABBRI

Amicus Illustrated is published by Amicus
P.O. Box 1329, Mankato, MN 56002
www.amicuspublishing.us

Library of Congress Cataloging-in-Publication Data
Meister, Cari, author.
 Do you really want to meet a tiger? / by Cari Meis-
ter ; illustrated by Daniele Fabbri.
    pages cm. — (Do you really want to meet?)
 Summary: "A child goes on an adventure to Russia
as a junior researcher to study tigers in the wild,
and learns about this endangered species"—
Provided by publisher.
 Audience: Grade K to 3.
 Includes bibliographical references and index.
 ISBN 978-1-60753-459-4 (library binding : alk.
paper) — ISBN 978-1-60753-674-1 (ebook)
 1. Tiger–Juvenile literature. 2. Russia (Federation—
Juvenile literature. I. Fabbri, Daniele, illustrator. II.
Title.
 QL737.C23M455 2015
 599.756–dc23   2013034703

Editor: Rebecca Glaser
Designer: Kathleen Petelinsek

Printed in the United States of America at
Corporate Graphics in North Mankato, Minnesota.
10 9 8 7 6 5 4 3 2

ABOUT THE AUTHOR

Cari Meister is the author of more than 120 books for children, including the *Tiny* series and *My Pony Jack*. She lives in Evergreen, CO and Minnetrista, MN with her husband, John, their four sons, one dog, one horse, and 4 hamsters. You can visit her online at www.carimeister.com.

ABOUT THE ILLUSTRATOR

Daniele Fabbri was born in Ravenna, Italy, in 1978. He graduated from Istituto Europeo di Design in Milan, Italy, and started his career as a cartoon animator, storyboarder, and background designer for animated series. He has worked as a freelance illustrator since 2003, collaborating with international publishers and advertising agencies.

Tiger cubs are playful and incredibly cute!
But have you seen their mama?

Yikes! That's one powerful feline. Glad we're on this side of the glass. Tigers have ravenous appetites. Some tigers eat up to 60 pounds (27 kg) of meat a day. Plus, tigers are the largest cats in the world. The largest tiger—the Siberian tiger—can weigh up to 660 pounds (300 kg). This Bengal tiger from India weighs about 300 pounds (136 kg).

Wait. *What did you say?*

You *really* want to meet a tiger? Not here in the zoo, but in the wild? Did you know that tigers are endangered? And they're extremely hard to find? You can't just find a wild tiger ANYWHERE.

But the zoo needs a junior researcher to study at a remote tiger reserve in eastern Russia. And you got the job! Pack your bags for a long trip!

It was a long plane ride, but here we are—the research station. For decades, wildlife biologists have been studying Siberian tigers here. They hope what they learn will help the tiger population grow.

LAST SIGHTING:

9

If you really want to meet a tiger, you have to
be patient. Scientists sometimes have to wait
weeks before seeing a tiger in the wild.

But you can look for clues. Do you have a log book?
Great. Write down signs of tigers, like: scratch
marks on trees, tracks in the snow, and . . .

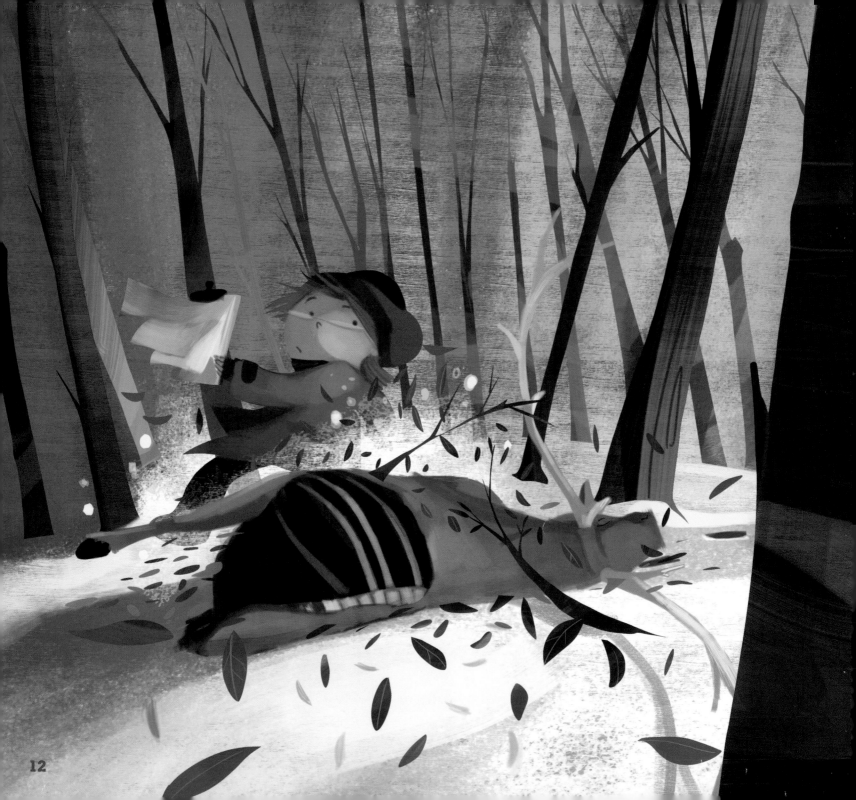

. . . a half-eaten elk! After a tiger makes a kill and eats its fill, the tiger covers the rest with branches, returning later to feast more.

Unfortunately, many times when scientists finally spot orange, they find only part of a tiger—a tuft of fur or a few bones. It's illegal to hunt tigers, but people do. Why? For money. Poaching is big business. Hunters sell tiger skins, bones, teeth, and claws for big bucks on the black market.

Most tigers are solitary. Even if you find one tiger, you most likely won't see two. Tigers have large territories, and guard them fiercely against other tigers. UNLESS . . .

. . . a tiger has cubs. In this case, her young will stay with
her about 18 months. The tigress does most of the hunting.

She uses her muscular limbs, sharp claws, and powerful jaws to catch her huge prey. Want to get closer?

No, I didn't think so. Let's take the helicopter and look for tigers from the air. Tigers are hard to find. Their stripes help them hide.

When you spot one, write down its location. The researchers will be glad for your help! The more they learn, the better chance they have of saving this endangered species.

WHERE DO TIGERS LIVE?

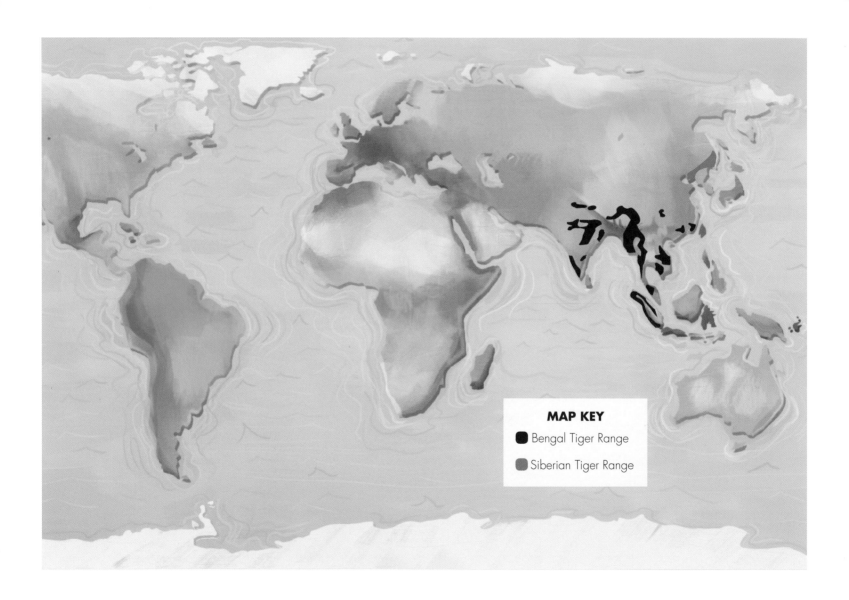

MAP KEY
- Bengal Tiger Range
- Siberian Tiger Range

GLOSSARY

endangered Near extinction; not many of one species left in the wild.

feline Belonging to the cat family.

poaching Illegal hunting of animals.

ravenous Very, very hungry.

reserve An area set aside to protect nature.

solitary Living alone, not in a group.

species A group of animals that share the same characteristics and that can produce offspring.

wildlife biologists Scientists that study wild animals.